50 Best-Ever Cookies and Biscuits

By: Kelly Johnson

Table of Contents

- Chocolate Chip Cookies
- Sugar Cookies
- Oatmeal Raisin Cookies
- Snickerdoodles
- Peanut Butter Cookies
- Shortbread Biscuits
- Gingerbread Cookies
- Double Chocolate Cookies
- Macadamia Nut Cookies
- Almond Biscotti
- Molasses Cookies
- Lemon Sugar Cookies
- Coconut Macaroons
- Chocolate Crinkle Cookies
- White Chocolate Cranberry Cookies
- Fortune Cookies
- Pecan Sandies
- Danish Butter Cookies
- Rugelach
- Raspberry Thumbprint Cookies
- Whoopie Pies
- Chocolate-Dipped Biscotti
- Brownie Cookies
- Chai-Spiced Cookies
- Caramel-Stuffed Cookies
- S'mores Cookies
- Italian Ricciarelli Cookies
- Lace Cookies
- Bourbon Biscuits
- Jammy Dodgers
- Anzac Biscuits
- Chocolate Hazelnut Cookies
- Peppermint Patties
- Honey Biscuits
- Spiced Molasses Cookies

- Nutella-Stuffed Cookies
- White Chocolate Macadamia Cookies
- Cherry Almond Cookies
- Pistachio Biscotti
- Maple Pecan Cookies
- Lemon Biscotti
- Cinnamon Roll Cookies
- Buttery Vanilla Bean Cookies
- Pumpkin Spice Cookies
- Chocolate Pudding Cookies
- Coconut-Lime Biscuits
- Pistachio-Rose Water Cookies
- Apple Cinnamon Cookies
- Salted Caramel Cookies
- Chocolate Toffee Cookies

Chocolate Chip Cookies

Ingredients:

- 2 1/4 cups all-purpose flour
- 1/2 tsp baking soda
- 1 cup unsalted butter, softened
- 1/2 cup granulated sugar
- 1 cup packed brown sugar
- 1 tsp vanilla extract
- 2 large eggs
- 2 cups semi-sweet chocolate chips
- 1/2 tsp salt

Instructions:

1. **Preheat the Oven:** Preheat your oven to 350°F (175°C).
2. **Mix Dry Ingredients:** In a bowl, whisk together the flour, baking soda, and salt.
3. **Cream Butter and Sugar:** In another bowl, beat together the softened butter, granulated sugar, and brown sugar until creamy. Add vanilla extract and eggs, one at a time, beating well after each addition.
4. **Combine Wet and Dry Ingredients:** Gradually mix in the dry ingredients until combined.
5. **Add Chocolate Chips:** Stir in the chocolate chips.
6. **Shape and Bake:** Drop tablespoonfuls of dough onto a baking sheet lined with parchment paper. Bake for 10-12 minutes, or until golden brown around the edges.
7. **Cool:** Allow the cookies to cool on the sheet for a few minutes before transferring to a wire rack to cool completely.

Sugar Cookies

Ingredients:

- 2 3/4 cups all-purpose flour
- 1 tsp baking soda
- 1/2 tsp baking powder
- 1 cup unsalted butter, softened
- 1 1/2 cups granulated sugar
- 1 large egg
- 1 tsp vanilla extract
- 1/2 tsp almond extract (optional)
- 1/4 cup granulated sugar (for rolling)

Instructions:

1. **Preheat the Oven:** Preheat your oven to 375°F (190°C).
2. **Mix Dry Ingredients:** In a small bowl, whisk together flour, baking soda, and baking powder.
3. **Cream Butter and Sugar:** In a large bowl, cream together the butter and 1 1/2 cups of sugar until light and fluffy. Beat in the egg and vanilla extract (and almond extract, if using).
4. **Combine Wet and Dry Ingredients:** Gradually add the dry ingredients to the wet ingredients, mixing until just combined.
5. **Shape Cookies:** Roll dough into 1-inch balls and then roll each ball in the 1/4 cup of sugar. Place on an ungreased baking sheet.
6. **Bake:** Bake for 8-10 minutes, or until the edges are golden. Allow to cool on a wire rack.

Oatmeal Raisin Cookies

Ingredients:

- 1 1/2 cups all-purpose flour
- 1 tsp baking soda
- 1 1/2 tsp ground cinnamon
- 1/2 tsp salt
- 1 cup unsalted butter, softened
- 3/4 cup granulated sugar
- 3/4 cup packed brown sugar
- 2 large eggs
- 1 tsp vanilla extract
- 3 cups old-fashioned rolled oats
- 1 1/2 cups raisins

Instructions:

1. **Preheat the Oven:** Preheat your oven to 350°F (175°C).
2. **Mix Dry Ingredients:** In a bowl, combine flour, baking soda, cinnamon, and salt.
3. **Cream Butter and Sugars:** In a large bowl, beat together the butter, granulated sugar, and brown sugar until light and fluffy. Add the eggs one at a time, then stir in the vanilla extract.
4. **Combine Wet and Dry Ingredients:** Gradually add the dry ingredients to the wet ingredients, mixing until just combined. Stir in the oats and raisins.
5. **Shape and Bake:** Drop tablespoonfuls of dough onto a baking sheet. Bake for 10-12 minutes, or until golden brown.
6. **Cool:** Allow cookies to cool on the baking sheet for a few minutes before transferring to a wire rack.

Snickerdoodles

Ingredients:

- 1 3/4 cups all-purpose flour
- 1 tsp cream of tartar
- 1/2 tsp baking soda
- 1/4 tsp salt
- 1/2 cup unsalted butter, softened
- 1 cup granulated sugar
- 2 large eggs
- 2 tbsp granulated sugar (for rolling)
- 2 tsp ground cinnamon (for rolling)

Instructions:

1. **Preheat the Oven:** Preheat your oven to 350°F (175°C).
2. **Mix Dry Ingredients:** In a bowl, whisk together the flour, cream of tartar, baking soda, and salt.
3. **Cream Butter and Sugar:** In a separate bowl, cream together the butter and sugar until light and fluffy. Add eggs, one at a time, beating well after each addition.
4. **Combine Wet and Dry Ingredients:** Gradually add the dry ingredients to the wet ingredients, mixing until combined.
5. **Shape Cookies:** In a small bowl, combine 2 tbsp sugar and cinnamon. Roll the dough into 1-inch balls and then roll in the cinnamon-sugar mixture. Place on an ungreased baking sheet.
6. **Bake:** Bake for 8-10 minutes, or until golden. Let cool on the baking sheet before transferring to a wire rack.

Peanut Butter Cookies

Ingredients:

- 1 cup peanut butter (smooth or crunchy)
- 1 cup granulated sugar
- 1 large egg
- 1 tsp vanilla extract
- 1/2 tsp baking soda (optional for more rise)

Instructions:

1. **Preheat the Oven:** Preheat your oven to 350°F (175°C).
2. **Mix Ingredients:** In a bowl, combine peanut butter, sugar, egg, vanilla extract, and baking soda (if using). Stir until smooth.
3. **Shape Cookies:** Roll dough into 1-inch balls and place on a baking sheet. Use a fork to flatten the cookies in a criss-cross pattern.
4. **Bake:** Bake for 8-10 minutes, or until lightly golden. Allow to cool on the baking sheet.

Shortbread Biscuits

Ingredients:

- 2 cups all-purpose flour
- 1/4 tsp salt
- 1 cup unsalted butter, softened
- 1/2 cup powdered sugar
- 1 tsp vanilla extract

Instructions:

1. **Preheat the Oven:** Preheat your oven to 350°F (175°C).
2. **Mix Ingredients:** In a bowl, cream together the butter and powdered sugar until smooth. Add the vanilla extract and mix. Gradually add the flour and salt, mixing until the dough comes together.
3. **Shape Biscuits:** Roll out the dough to about 1/4-inch thick. Cut into shapes using cookie cutters or into rectangles.
4. **Bake:** Place on a baking sheet and bake for 10-12 minutes or until the edges are lightly golden. Cool on a wire rack.

Gingerbread Cookies

Ingredients:

- 3 1/4 cups all-purpose flour
- 1 tsp baking soda
- 2 tsp ground ginger
- 1 tsp ground cinnamon
- 1/2 tsp ground cloves
- 1/2 tsp salt
- 1 cup unsalted butter, softened
- 1/2 cup brown sugar, packed
- 1 large egg
- 1/2 cup molasses

Instructions:

1. **Preheat the Oven:** Preheat your oven to 350°F (175°C).
2. **Mix Dry Ingredients:** In a bowl, whisk together flour, baking soda, ginger, cinnamon, cloves, and salt.
3. **Cream Butter and Sugar:** In a separate bowl, beat together butter and brown sugar until fluffy. Add the egg and molasses, and mix until combined.
4. **Combine Wet and Dry Ingredients:** Gradually add the dry ingredients to the wet ingredients, mixing until smooth.
5. **Roll and Cut:** Roll out dough to 1/4-inch thickness and cut into desired shapes. Place on a baking sheet.
6. **Bake:** Bake for 8-10 minutes, or until firm. Cool on a wire rack.

Double Chocolate Cookies

Ingredients:

- 1 3/4 cups all-purpose flour
- 1/2 cup unsweetened cocoa powder
- 1 tsp baking powder
- 1/2 tsp salt
- 1 cup unsalted butter, softened
- 1 1/2 cups granulated sugar
- 2 large eggs
- 1 tsp vanilla extract
- 2 cups semi-sweet chocolate chips

Instructions:

1. **Preheat the Oven:** Preheat your oven to 350°F (175°C).
2. **Mix Dry Ingredients:** In a bowl, whisk together flour, cocoa powder, baking powder, and salt.
3. **Cream Butter and Sugar:** In another bowl, beat together butter and sugar until fluffy. Add eggs, one at a time, then mix in vanilla.
4. **Combine Wet and Dry Ingredients:** Gradually add the dry ingredients to the wet ingredients. Stir in chocolate chips.
5. **Shape and Bake:** Drop tablespoonfuls of dough onto a baking sheet and bake for 10-12 minutes. Cool on a wire rack.

Macadamia Nut Cookies

Ingredients:

- 2 1/4 cups all-purpose flour
- 1 tsp baking soda
- 1/2 tsp salt
- 1 cup unsalted butter, softened
- 1 cup granulated sugar
- 1 cup packed brown sugar
- 2 large eggs
- 1 tsp vanilla extract
- 2 cups macadamia nuts, coarsely chopped
- 1 1/2 cups white chocolate chips

Instructions:

1. **Preheat the Oven:** Preheat your oven to 350°F (175°C).
2. **Mix Dry Ingredients:** In a bowl, combine flour, baking soda, and salt.
3. **Cream Butter and Sugars:** In a separate bowl, beat together butter, granulated sugar, and brown sugar until smooth. Add eggs and vanilla extract.
4. **Combine Wet and Dry Ingredients:** Gradually mix in the dry ingredients. Stir in the macadamia nuts and white chocolate chips.
5. **Shape and Bake:** Drop spoonfuls of dough onto a baking sheet and bake for 10-12 minutes. Cool on a wire rack.

Almond Biscotti

Ingredients:

- 2 cups all-purpose flour
- 1 tsp baking powder
- 1/2 tsp salt
- 1 cup granulated sugar
- 2 large eggs
- 1 tsp vanilla extract
- 1 tsp almond extract
- 1 1/2 cups whole almonds, toasted and coarsely chopped

Instructions:

1. **Preheat the Oven:** Preheat your oven to 350°F (175°C).
2. **Mix Dry Ingredients:** In a bowl, combine the flour, baking powder, and salt.
3. **Make the Dough:** In a separate bowl, beat together sugar and eggs until light and fluffy. Add vanilla and almond extracts. Gradually add dry ingredients and mix until combined. Stir in the almonds.
4. **Shape and Bake:** Divide the dough into two logs and place on a parchment-lined baking sheet. Bake for 25-30 minutes until firm and lightly golden.
5. **Slice and Bake Again:** Let the logs cool for 10 minutes, then slice them diagonally into 1/2-inch thick pieces. Place the slices back on the baking sheet and bake for another 10-12 minutes to crisp up.
6. **Cool:** Cool completely on a wire rack.

Molasses Cookies

Ingredients:

- 2 1/4 cups all-purpose flour
- 1 tsp baking soda
- 1 tsp ground ginger
- 1 tsp ground cinnamon
- 1/4 tsp ground cloves
- 1/4 tsp salt
- 3/4 cup unsalted butter, softened
- 1 cup packed brown sugar
- 1 large egg
- 1/4 cup molasses
- 1/4 cup granulated sugar (for rolling)

Instructions:

1. **Preheat the Oven:** Preheat your oven to 350°F (175°C).
2. **Mix Dry Ingredients:** In a bowl, whisk together the flour, baking soda, ginger, cinnamon, cloves, and salt.
3. **Cream Butter and Sugar:** In a large bowl, beat together the butter and brown sugar until fluffy. Add the egg and molasses, and beat until combined.
4. **Combine Wet and Dry Ingredients:** Gradually add the dry ingredients to the wet ingredients and mix until smooth.
5. **Shape and Roll:** Roll dough into 1-inch balls and roll in the granulated sugar. Place on a baking sheet.
6. **Bake:** Bake for 8-10 minutes or until the edges are set and the tops crack. Cool on a wire rack.

Lemon Sugar Cookies

Ingredients:

- 2 3/4 cups all-purpose flour
- 1 tsp baking soda
- 1/2 tsp salt
- 1 cup unsalted butter, softened
- 1 1/2 cups granulated sugar, divided
- 1 large egg
- 1 tbsp lemon zest
- 2 tbsp fresh lemon juice
- 1/4 cup sugar (for rolling)

Instructions:

1. **Preheat the Oven:** Preheat your oven to 350°F (175°C).
2. **Mix Dry Ingredients:** In a bowl, whisk together the flour, baking soda, and salt.
3. **Cream Butter and Sugar:** In a large bowl, beat together the butter and 1 1/2 cups sugar until creamy. Add egg, lemon zest, and lemon juice, mixing until smooth.
4. **Combine Wet and Dry Ingredients:** Gradually add the dry ingredients and mix until combined.
5. **Shape and Roll:** Roll dough into 1-inch balls, then roll in the 1/4 cup sugar. Place on a baking sheet.
6. **Bake:** Bake for 8-10 minutes or until edges are golden. Cool on a wire rack.

Coconut Macaroons

Ingredients:

- 2 1/2 cups sweetened shredded coconut
- 1/2 cup sweetened condensed milk
- 1/4 tsp vanilla extract
- 2 large egg whites
- 1/4 tsp salt

Instructions:

1. **Preheat the Oven:** Preheat your oven to 325°F (165°C).
2. **Mix Coconut and Milk:** In a bowl, combine the coconut, condensed milk, and vanilla extract.
3. **Whip Egg Whites:** In a separate bowl, beat the egg whites and salt until stiff peaks form.
4. **Fold Together:** Gently fold the whipped egg whites into the coconut mixture.
5. **Shape and Bake:** Drop tablespoonfuls of the mixture onto a baking sheet. Bake for 12-15 minutes or until golden brown.
6. **Cool:** Allow macaroons to cool on a wire rack.

Chocolate Crinkle Cookies

Ingredients:

- 1 1/2 cups all-purpose flour
- 1 tsp baking powder
- 1/4 tsp salt
- 1/2 cup unsweetened cocoa powder
- 1/2 cup granulated sugar
- 1/2 cup packed brown sugar
- 2 large eggs
- 1/2 cup vegetable oil
- 1 tsp vanilla extract
- 1/2 cup powdered sugar (for rolling)

Instructions:

1. **Preheat the Oven:** Preheat your oven to 350°F (175°C).
2. **Mix Dry Ingredients:** In a bowl, whisk together the flour, baking powder, salt, and cocoa powder.
3. **Combine Wet Ingredients:** In a large bowl, beat together granulated sugar, brown sugar, eggs, oil, and vanilla until smooth.
4. **Combine Wet and Dry Ingredients:** Gradually add the dry ingredients and mix until combined.
5. **Shape and Roll:** Roll dough into 1-inch balls, then roll in powdered sugar. Place on a baking sheet.
6. **Bake:** Bake for 10-12 minutes, or until the cookies are cracked and slightly puffed. Cool on a wire rack.

White Chocolate Cranberry Cookies

Ingredients:

- 2 cups all-purpose flour
- 1 tsp baking soda
- 1/2 tsp salt
- 1/2 cup unsalted butter, softened
- 3/4 cup granulated sugar
- 1/2 cup packed brown sugar
- 2 large eggs
- 1 tsp vanilla extract
- 1 cup dried cranberries
- 1 cup white chocolate chips

Instructions:

1. **Preheat the Oven:** Preheat your oven to 350°F (175°C).
2. **Mix Dry Ingredients:** In a bowl, whisk together the flour, baking soda, and salt.
3. **Cream Butter and Sugars:** In a large bowl, beat together the butter, granulated sugar, and brown sugar until smooth. Add the eggs and vanilla, mixing until combined.
4. **Combine Wet and Dry Ingredients:** Gradually add the dry ingredients and mix. Stir in the cranberries and white chocolate chips.
5. **Shape and Bake:** Drop spoonfuls of dough onto a baking sheet. Bake for 10-12 minutes, or until the cookies are golden brown.
6. **Cool:** Cool on a wire rack.

Fortune Cookies

Ingredients:

- 1/2 cup all-purpose flour
- 1/2 cup granulated sugar
- 2 large egg whites
- 1 tsp vanilla extract
- 1 tsp almond extract
- 1/4 tsp salt
- 1/4 cup water

Instructions:

1. **Preheat the Oven:** Preheat your oven to 375°F (190°C).
2. **Mix Ingredients:** In a bowl, combine flour, sugar, egg whites, vanilla extract, almond extract, salt, and water. Stir until smooth.
3. **Bake:** Drop spoonfuls of dough onto a baking sheet lined with parchment paper. Spread into thin 3-inch circles.
4. **Shape Cookies:** Bake for 7-8 minutes, or until the edges are golden. Working quickly, place a fortune in each cookie and fold it in half, then bend it over the edge of a cup to shape.
5. **Cool:** Let cool completely.

Pecan Sandies

Ingredients:

- 2 cups all-purpose flour
- 1/4 tsp salt
- 1 cup unsalted butter, softened
- 1/2 cup powdered sugar
- 1 tsp vanilla extract
- 1 cup chopped pecans

Instructions:

1. **Preheat the Oven:** Preheat your oven to 350°F (175°C).
2. **Mix Dry Ingredients:** In a bowl, whisk together the flour and salt.
3. **Cream Butter and Sugar:** In a large bowl, beat together the butter and powdered sugar until light and fluffy. Add the vanilla extract.
4. **Combine Wet and Dry Ingredients:** Gradually add the dry ingredients and mix until combined. Stir in the pecans.
5. **Shape and Bake:** Roll dough into 1-inch balls and place on a baking sheet. Flatten with a fork. Bake for 10-12 minutes or until golden brown.
6. **Cool:** Cool on a wire rack.

Danish Butter Cookies

Ingredients:

- 2 1/2 cups all-purpose flour
- 1/2 tsp salt
- 1 cup unsalted butter, softened
- 1/2 cup granulated sugar
- 1 large egg
- 1 tsp vanilla extract

Instructions:

1. **Preheat the Oven:** Preheat your oven to 350°F (175°C).
2. **Mix Dry Ingredients:** In a bowl, whisk together the flour and salt.
3. **Cream Butter and Sugar:** In a large bowl, beat together the butter and sugar until light and fluffy. Add the egg and vanilla extract and mix.
4. **Combine Wet and Dry Ingredients:** Gradually add the dry ingredients and mix until combined.
5. **Shape and Bake:** Drop spoonfuls of dough onto a baking sheet. Bake for 10-12 minutes or until golden.
6. **Cool:** Let cool on a wire rack.

Rugelach

Ingredients:

- 2 cups all-purpose flour
- 1/4 tsp salt
- 1 cup unsalted butter, cold and cut into pieces
- 8 oz cream cheese, cold and cut into pieces
- 1/4 cup granulated sugar
- 1 tsp vanilla extract
- 1/2 cup granulated sugar (for rolling)
- 1/2 cup chopped walnuts or pecans
- 1/2 cup fruit preserves (apricot, raspberry, or strawberry)
- 1/4 cup powdered sugar

Instructions:

1. **Preheat the Oven:** Preheat your oven to 350°F (175°C).
2. **Make Dough:** In a food processor, pulse the flour, salt, butter, cream cheese, sugar, and vanilla until dough forms.
3. **Chill Dough:** Wrap dough in plastic wrap and refrigerate for at least 30 minutes.
4. **Assemble Rugelach:** Roll out dough on a floured surface. Spread a thin layer of preserves, sprinkle with sugar and nuts. Cut dough into wedges and roll each into a crescent shape.
5. **Bake:** Place on a baking sheet and bake for 20-25 minutes or until golden.
6. **Cool:** Dust with powdered sugar and let cool.

Raspberry Thumbprint Cookies

Ingredients:

- 2 1/4 cups all-purpose flour
- 1/2 tsp baking powder
- 1/4 tsp salt
- 1 cup unsalted butter, softened
- 1/2 cup granulated sugar
- 1 large egg yolk
- 1 tsp vanilla extract
- 1/4 cup raspberry jam (or your preferred fruit jam)

Instructions:

1. **Preheat the Oven:** Preheat your oven to 350°F (175°C).
2. **Mix Dry Ingredients:** In a bowl, whisk together the flour, baking powder, and salt.
3. **Cream Butter and Sugar:** In a separate bowl, beat together the butter and sugar until light and fluffy. Add the egg yolk and vanilla extract, and mix until combined.
4. **Combine Wet and Dry Ingredients:** Gradually add the dry ingredients and mix until just combined.
5. **Shape Cookies:** Roll dough into 1-inch balls and place them on a parchment-lined baking sheet. Use your thumb to make a small indentation in the center of each cookie.
6. **Add Jam:** Spoon a small amount of raspberry jam into each indentation.
7. **Bake:** Bake for 10-12 minutes, or until the edges are golden. Cool on a wire rack.

Whoopie Pies

Ingredients:

- **For the Cake:**
    - 1 1/2 cups all-purpose flour
    - 1/2 cup cocoa powder
    - 1 tsp baking powder
    - 1/2 tsp baking soda
    - 1/4 tsp salt
    - 1/2 cup unsalted butter, softened
    - 1 cup granulated sugar
    - 1 large egg
    - 1 tsp vanilla extract
    - 1 cup buttermilk
- **For the Filling:**
    - 1/2 cup unsalted butter, softened
    - 1 1/2 cups powdered sugar
    - 1/2 tsp vanilla extract
    - 1/2 cup marshmallow fluff

Instructions:

1. **Preheat the Oven:** Preheat your oven to 350°F (175°C). Line two baking sheets with parchment paper.
2. **Make the Cake Batter:** In a bowl, whisk together flour, cocoa powder, baking powder, baking soda, and salt. In another bowl, beat butter and sugar until light and fluffy. Add the egg and vanilla extract, mixing until combined. Gradually add the dry ingredients, alternating with the buttermilk.
3. **Scoop and Bake:** Drop tablespoonfuls of dough onto the baking sheets. Bake for 10-12 minutes, or until a toothpick comes out clean. Cool on a wire rack.
4. **Make the Filling:** Beat together the butter, powdered sugar, vanilla, and marshmallow fluff until smooth.
5. **Assemble the Whoopie Pies:** Spread a generous amount of filling on the flat side of one cookie and top with another cookie, pressing gently to sandwich them together. Let cool.

Chocolate-Dipped Biscotti

Ingredients:

- 2 cups all-purpose flour
- 1 tsp baking powder
- 1/4 tsp salt
- 1/2 cup granulated sugar
- 3 large eggs
- 1 tsp vanilla extract
- 1/2 cup mini chocolate chips
- 4 oz semisweet chocolate, melted (for dipping)

Instructions:

1. **Preheat the Oven:** Preheat your oven to 350°F (175°C). Line a baking sheet with parchment paper.
2. **Mix Dry Ingredients:** In a bowl, whisk together the flour, baking powder, salt, and sugar.
3. **Add Wet Ingredients:** In another bowl, beat the eggs and vanilla extract. Gradually add the wet ingredients to the dry ingredients and mix until combined. Stir in the mini chocolate chips.
4. **Shape and Bake:** Shape the dough into a log on the baking sheet. Bake for 25-30 minutes until golden brown.
5. **Slice and Bake Again:** Let the log cool for 10 minutes, then slice into 1/2-inch thick pieces. Place the slices back on the baking sheet and bake for an additional 10-12 minutes until crisp.
6. **Dip in Chocolate:** Let the biscotti cool completely before dipping one end in the melted chocolate. Allow the chocolate to set before serving.

Brownie Cookies

Ingredients:

- 1 cup semisweet chocolate chips
- 1/2 cup unsalted butter
- 1 cup granulated sugar
- 2 large eggs
- 1 tsp vanilla extract
- 1 cup all-purpose flour
- 1/4 tsp salt
- 1/2 tsp baking powder

Instructions:

1. **Preheat the Oven:** Preheat your oven to 350°F (175°C). Line a baking sheet with parchment paper.
2. **Melt Chocolate and Butter:** In a bowl, melt the chocolate chips and butter together in the microwave or over a double boiler, stirring until smooth.
3. **Mix Ingredients:** In a separate bowl, beat the sugar, eggs, and vanilla extract until fluffy. Add the melted chocolate mixture and mix until combined. Gradually add flour, salt, and baking powder.
4. **Scoop and Bake:** Drop spoonfuls of dough onto the baking sheet. Bake for 10-12 minutes, or until the edges are set. Cool on a wire rack.

Chai-Spiced Cookies

Ingredients:

- 2 cups all-purpose flour
- 1 tsp ground cinnamon
- 1/2 tsp ground ginger
- 1/2 tsp ground cardamom
- 1/4 tsp ground cloves
- 1/2 tsp baking soda
- 1/2 tsp salt
- 3/4 cup unsalted butter, softened
- 1 cup brown sugar
- 1 large egg
- 1 tsp vanilla extract
- 1 tbsp milk

Instructions:

1. **Preheat the Oven:** Preheat your oven to 350°F (175°C). Line a baking sheet with parchment paper.
2. **Mix Dry Ingredients:** In a bowl, whisk together the flour, cinnamon, ginger, cardamom, cloves, baking soda, and salt.
3. **Cream Butter and Sugar:** In a large bowl, beat the butter and brown sugar until light and fluffy. Add the egg, vanilla extract, and milk, and mix until smooth.
4. **Combine Wet and Dry Ingredients:** Gradually add the dry ingredients to the wet mixture and stir until just combined.
5. **Shape and Bake:** Roll dough into 1-inch balls and place on the baking sheet. Bake for 10-12 minutes, or until edges are golden. Cool on a wire rack.

Caramel-Stuffed Cookies

Ingredients:

- 2 cups all-purpose flour
- 1 tsp baking soda
- 1/2 tsp salt
- 1 cup unsalted butter, softened
- 1 cup brown sugar
- 1 large egg
- 1 tsp vanilla extract
- 24 caramel candies (unwrapped)

Instructions:

1. **Preheat the Oven:** Preheat your oven to 350°F (175°C). Line a baking sheet with parchment paper.
2. **Make Dough:** In a bowl, whisk together the flour, baking soda, and salt. In another bowl, beat the butter and brown sugar until creamy. Add the egg and vanilla, and mix until combined. Gradually add the dry ingredients and mix until smooth.
3. **Stuff the Cookies:** Scoop a small amount of dough and flatten it in your hand. Place a caramel candy in the center and fold the dough around it, sealing it completely.
4. **Bake:** Place on the baking sheet and bake for 10-12 minutes or until golden brown. Cool on a wire rack.

S'mores Cookies

Ingredients:

- 1 1/2 cups all-purpose flour
- 1/2 tsp baking soda
- 1/2 tsp salt
- 1/2 cup unsalted butter, softened
- 1 cup granulated sugar
- 1 large egg
- 1 tsp vanilla extract
- 1 cup mini marshmallows
- 1/2 cup chocolate chips
- 1/2 cup graham cracker crumbs

Instructions:

1. **Preheat the Oven:** Preheat your oven to 350°F (175°C). Line a baking sheet with parchment paper.
2. **Mix Dry Ingredients:** In a bowl, whisk together the flour, baking soda, and salt.
3. **Cream Butter and Sugar:** In a large bowl, beat the butter and sugar until light and fluffy. Add the egg and vanilla extract and mix.
4. **Combine Wet and Dry Ingredients:** Gradually add the dry ingredients and stir in the marshmallows, chocolate chips, and graham cracker crumbs.
5. **Shape and Bake:** Drop spoonfuls of dough onto the baking sheet. Bake for 8-10 minutes or until golden brown. Cool on a wire rack.

Italian Ricciarelli Cookies

Ingredients:

- 2 cups almond flour
- 1 cup powdered sugar
- 2 large egg whites
- 1 tsp almond extract
- 1/4 tsp salt
- 1/4 cup granulated sugar

Instructions:

1. **Preheat the Oven:** Preheat your oven to 325°F (165°C). Line a baking sheet with parchment paper.
2. **Mix Ingredients:** In a bowl, combine almond flour, powdered sugar, egg whites, almond extract, and salt. Stir until a sticky dough forms.
3. **Shape Cookies:** Roll dough into 1-inch balls and then flatten slightly. Place on the baking sheet.
4. **Bake:** Bake for 12-15 minutes, or until slightly golden around the edges. Let cool before dusting with powdered sugar.

Lace Cookies

Ingredients:

- 1/2 cup unsalted butter
- 1 cup granulated sugar
- 2 tbsp all-purpose flour
- 1 tbsp heavy cream
- 1 tsp vanilla extract
- 1/4 tsp salt
- 1/2 cup sliced almonds

Instructions:

1. **Preheat the Oven:** Preheat your oven to 350°F (175°C). Line a baking sheet with parchment paper.
2. **Make Dough:** In a saucepan, melt butter with sugar, flour, cream, vanilla, and salt. Stir constantly until smooth.
3. **Add Almonds:** Stir in the sliced almonds.
4. **Shape and Bake:** Drop teaspoonfuls of dough onto the baking sheet. Bake for 6-8 minutes, or until golden brown. Let cool completely before removing from the baking sheet.

Bourbon Biscuits

Ingredients:

- **For the Biscuit:**
    - 1 3/4 cups all-purpose flour
    - 1/4 cup cocoa powder
    - 1/2 tsp baking powder
    - 1/4 tsp salt
    - 1/2 cup unsalted butter, softened
    - 1/2 cup caster sugar
    - 1 large egg
    - 1 tsp vanilla extract
    - 1 tbsp milk
- **For the Filling:**
    - 1/2 cup powdered sugar
    - 2 tbsp unsalted butter, softened
    - 1 tbsp cocoa powder
    - 1 tsp vanilla extract

Instructions:

1. **Preheat the Oven:** Preheat your oven to 350°F (175°C). Line a baking sheet with parchment paper.
2. **Make the Biscuit Dough:** In a bowl, whisk together the flour, cocoa powder, baking powder, and salt. In a separate bowl, beat the butter and sugar until light and fluffy. Add the egg, vanilla extract, and milk, and mix until combined. Gradually add the dry ingredients and mix until a dough forms.
3. **Shape and Bake:** Roll the dough out to 1/8-inch thickness. Use a cookie cutter to cut out rectangular shapes. Place them on the baking sheet and bake for 10-12 minutes. Allow to cool completely.
4. **Make the Filling:** Beat together the powdered sugar, butter, cocoa powder, and vanilla extract until smooth.
5. **Assemble the Biscuits:** Spread a generous amount of filling on one biscuit and sandwich it with another. Allow to set before serving.

Jammy Dodgers

Ingredients:

- 2 cups all-purpose flour
- 1/2 cup unsalted butter, softened
- 1/2 cup caster sugar
- 1 large egg
- 1 tsp vanilla extract
- 1/4 tsp salt
- 1/4 cup raspberry jam (or your preferred jam)

Instructions:

1. **Preheat the Oven:** Preheat your oven to 350°F (175°C). Line a baking sheet with parchment paper.
2. **Make the Dough:** In a bowl, beat the butter and sugar until creamy. Add the egg and vanilla extract and mix until smooth. Gradually add the flour and salt until a dough forms. Wrap the dough in plastic wrap and refrigerate for 30 minutes.
3. **Shape the Biscuits:** Roll the dough out on a floured surface to about 1/8-inch thickness. Use a round cutter to cut out circles. Use a smaller cutter to cut a hole in half of the circles to create the "jammy" effect.
4. **Bake:** Place the biscuits on the baking sheet and bake for 8-10 minutes until golden brown. Cool completely.
5. **Assemble:** Spread a little raspberry jam on the solid biscuits and sandwich with the ones with holes. Dust with powdered sugar before serving.

Anzac Biscuits

Ingredients:

- 1 1/2 cups rolled oats
- 1 cup desiccated coconut
- 1 cup all-purpose flour
- 3/4 cup caster sugar
- 1/2 cup unsalted butter
- 2 tbsp golden syrup
- 1/2 tsp baking soda
- 1 tbsp boiling water

Instructions:

1. **Preheat the Oven:** Preheat your oven to 350°F (175°C). Line a baking sheet with parchment paper.
2. **Make the Dough:** In a bowl, combine oats, coconut, flour, and sugar. In a separate pan, melt the butter and golden syrup together over low heat. In a small bowl, dissolve the baking soda in boiling water and add it to the melted butter mixture.
3. **Combine:** Pour the wet mixture into the dry ingredients and mix until combined.
4. **Shape and Bake:** Roll tablespoon-sized amounts of dough into balls and flatten them slightly on the baking sheet. Bake for 10-12 minutes or until golden brown. Allow to cool on a wire rack.

Chocolate Hazelnut Cookies

Ingredients:

- 1 1/2 cups all-purpose flour
- 1/2 tsp baking soda
- 1/4 tsp salt
- 1/2 cup unsalted butter, softened
- 1 cup granulated sugar
- 1 large egg
- 1 tsp vanilla extract
- 1/2 cup chocolate hazelnut spread (such as Nutella)
- 1/2 cup chopped hazelnuts
- 1/2 cup chocolate chips

Instructions:

1. **Preheat the Oven:** Preheat your oven to 350°F (175°C). Line a baking sheet with parchment paper.
2. **Make the Dough:** In a bowl, whisk together the flour, baking soda, and salt. In a separate bowl, beat the butter and sugar until light and fluffy. Add the egg and vanilla extract and mix. Stir in the chocolate hazelnut spread until combined.
3. **Add Nuts and Chips:** Mix in the chopped hazelnuts and chocolate chips.
4. **Shape and Bake:** Drop tablespoonfuls of dough onto the baking sheet and bake for 8-10 minutes, or until golden brown. Allow to cool on a wire rack.

Peppermint Patties

Ingredients:

- 2 cups powdered sugar
- 2 cups dark chocolate chips
- 1/4 cup unsweetened cocoa powder
- 1/4 cup corn syrup
- 2 tbsp unsalted butter, softened
- 1/2 tsp peppermint extract
- 1 tbsp milk

Instructions:

1. **Make the Peppermint Filling:** In a bowl, mix together powdered sugar, cocoa powder, corn syrup, butter, peppermint extract, and milk until smooth. Roll into small balls and flatten into discs.
2. **Chill:** Place the discs on a parchment-lined baking sheet and refrigerate for 30 minutes.
3. **Dip in Chocolate:** Melt the chocolate chips in a heatproof bowl over a double boiler. Dip each peppermint patty into the melted chocolate and return to the baking sheet.
4. **Cool:** Allow to cool and set before serving.

Honey Biscuits

Ingredients:

- 2 cups all-purpose flour
- 1/2 cup unsalted butter, softened
- 1/2 cup honey
- 1/4 cup granulated sugar
- 1 large egg
- 1 tsp vanilla extract
- 1/4 tsp salt

Instructions:

1. **Preheat the Oven:** Preheat your oven to 350°F (175°C). Line a baking sheet with parchment paper.
2. **Make the Dough:** In a bowl, beat the butter and sugar until light and fluffy. Add the egg, vanilla extract, and honey, and mix until smooth. Gradually add the flour and salt until a dough forms.
3. **Shape and Bake:** Roll dough into small balls and place them on the baking sheet. Flatten with a fork. Bake for 8-10 minutes or until golden brown. Cool on a wire rack.

Spiced Molasses Cookies

Ingredients:

- 2 1/4 cups all-purpose flour
- 1 1/2 tsp ground ginger
- 1 tsp ground cinnamon
- 1/2 tsp ground cloves
- 1/2 tsp ground nutmeg
- 1/2 tsp baking soda
- 1/4 tsp salt
- 3/4 cup unsalted butter, softened
- 1 cup granulated sugar
- 1/4 cup molasses
- 1 large egg
- 1/4 cup granulated sugar (for rolling)

Instructions:

1. **Preheat the Oven:** Preheat your oven to 350°F (175°C). Line a baking sheet with parchment paper.
2. **Make the Dough:** In a bowl, whisk together flour, spices, baking soda, and salt. In another bowl, beat the butter and sugar until light and fluffy. Add molasses and egg, and mix until combined. Gradually add the dry ingredients and mix until a dough forms.
3. **Shape and Bake:** Roll dough into balls and roll in sugar. Place on the baking sheet and bake for 8-10 minutes. Cool on a wire rack.

Nutella-Stuffed Cookies

Ingredients:

- 2 cups all-purpose flour
- 1 tsp baking soda
- 1/2 tsp salt
- 1 cup unsalted butter, softened
- 1 cup brown sugar
- 1/2 cup granulated sugar
- 2 large eggs
- 1 tsp vanilla extract
- 1/2 cup Nutella
- 1/2 cup chocolate chips

Instructions:

1. **Preheat the Oven:** Preheat your oven to 350°F (175°C). Line a baking sheet with parchment paper.
2. **Make the Dough:** In a bowl, whisk together the flour, baking soda, and salt. In a separate bowl, beat the butter and sugars until light and fluffy. Add the eggs and vanilla extract and mix until smooth.
3. **Stuff the Cookies:** Take a tablespoon of dough, flatten it, and place a teaspoon of Nutella in the center. Wrap the dough around the Nutella and roll into a ball. Place on the baking sheet and top with chocolate chips.
4. **Bake:** Bake for 8-10 minutes or until golden brown. Allow to cool on a wire rack.

White Chocolate Macadamia Cookies

Ingredients:

- 2 cups all-purpose flour
- 1/2 tsp baking soda
- 1/4 tsp salt
- 1 cup unsalted butter, softened
- 3/4 cup granulated sugar
- 3/4 cup packed brown sugar
- 1 tsp vanilla extract
- 2 large eggs
- 1 cup white chocolate chips
- 1 cup macadamia nuts, chopped

Instructions:

1. **Preheat the Oven:** Preheat your oven to 350°F (175°C). Line a baking sheet with parchment paper.
2. **Make the Dough:** In a bowl, whisk together flour, baking soda, and salt. In a separate bowl, beat the butter and sugars until light and fluffy. Add the eggs and vanilla extract, and mix until smooth.
3. **Add Chips and Nuts:** Stir in white chocolate chips and chopped macadamia nuts.
4. **Shape and Bake:** Drop tablespoonfuls of dough onto the baking sheet. Bake for 8-10 minutes or until golden brown. Let cool before serving.

Cherry Almond Cookies

Ingredients:

- 1 1/2 cups all-purpose flour
- 1/2 tsp baking powder
- 1/4 tsp salt
- 1/2 cup unsalted butter, softened
- 1 cup granulated sugar
- 1 large egg
- 1 tsp almond extract
- 1/2 cup maraschino cherries, chopped
- 1/2 cup sliced almonds

Instructions:

1. **Preheat the Oven:** Preheat your oven to 350°F (175°C). Line a baking sheet with parchment paper.
2. **Make the Dough:** In a bowl, whisk together the flour, baking powder, and salt. In another bowl, beat the butter and sugar until light and fluffy. Add the egg and almond extract, and mix until smooth.
3. **Add Cherries and Almonds:** Stir in the chopped cherries and sliced almonds.
4. **Shape and Bake:** Drop tablespoonfuls of dough onto the baking sheet. Bake for 8-10 minutes or until golden brown. Let cool on a wire rack.

Pistachio Biscotti

Ingredients:

- 2 cups all-purpose flour
- 1 tsp baking powder
- 1/2 tsp salt
- 1 cup shelled pistachios, chopped
- 1/2 cup granulated sugar
- 2 large eggs
- 1 tsp vanilla extract
- 1/2 tsp almond extract
- 1/4 cup unsalted butter, melted

Instructions:

1. **Preheat the Oven:** Preheat your oven to 350°F (175°C). Line a baking sheet with parchment paper.
2. **Make the Dough:** In a bowl, whisk together the flour, baking powder, and salt. Stir in the pistachios. In another bowl, beat the eggs, sugar, vanilla, and almond extract until smooth. Add the wet ingredients to the dry ingredients along with the melted butter. Mix to form a dough.
3. **Shape and Bake:** Divide the dough into two logs and place them on the baking sheet. Bake for 25-30 minutes until golden brown. Allow to cool for 10 minutes, then slice the logs into 1/2-inch slices.
4. **Second Bake:** Place the sliced biscotti back on the baking sheet and bake for an additional 10 minutes, flipping halfway through, until crisp. Cool completely before serving.

Maple Pecan Cookies

Ingredients:

- 1 1/2 cups all-purpose flour
- 1/2 tsp baking soda
- 1/4 tsp salt
- 1/2 cup unsalted butter, softened
- 1/2 cup maple syrup
- 1/4 cup brown sugar, packed
- 1 large egg
- 1 tsp vanilla extract
- 1 cup pecans, chopped

Instructions:

1. **Preheat the Oven:** Preheat your oven to 350°F (175°C). Line a baking sheet with parchment paper.
2. **Make the Dough:** In a bowl, whisk together the flour, baking soda, and salt. In another bowl, beat the butter, maple syrup, and brown sugar until smooth. Add the egg and vanilla extract, and mix until combined. Gradually add the dry ingredients and mix until a dough forms. Stir in the chopped pecans.
3. **Shape and Bake:** Drop spoonfuls of dough onto the baking sheet. Bake for 10-12 minutes until golden brown. Let cool on a wire rack.

Lemon Biscotti

Ingredients:

- 2 cups all-purpose flour
- 1 tsp baking powder
- 1/4 tsp salt
- 1/2 cup granulated sugar
- 2 large eggs
- 1 tsp vanilla extract
- 1 tbsp lemon zest
- 1/2 cup lemon juice
- 1/2 cup sliced almonds (optional)

Instructions:

1. **Preheat the Oven:** Preheat your oven to 350°F (175°C). Line a baking sheet with parchment paper.
2. **Make the Dough:** In a bowl, whisk together the flour, baking powder, and salt. In another bowl, beat the eggs and sugar until pale and creamy. Add the vanilla extract, lemon zest, and lemon juice, and mix. Gradually add the dry ingredients and mix until a dough forms. Stir in the almonds if using.
3. **Shape and Bake:** Divide the dough into two logs and place them on the baking sheet. Bake for 25-30 minutes, until golden. Let cool for 10 minutes, then slice into 1/2-inch pieces.
4. **Second Bake:** Arrange the biscotti on the baking sheet and bake for an additional 10 minutes, flipping halfway through, until crisp. Cool completely before serving.

Cinnamon Roll Cookies

Ingredients:

- 2 1/4 cups all-purpose flour
- 1/2 tsp baking soda
- 1/2 tsp salt
- 1 cup unsalted butter, softened
- 1 cup granulated sugar
- 1 large egg
- 1 tsp vanilla extract
- 1 tsp ground cinnamon
- 1/4 cup brown sugar, packed

Instructions:

1. **Preheat the Oven:** Preheat your oven to 350°F (175°C). Line a baking sheet with parchment paper.
2. **Make the Dough:** In a bowl, whisk together the flour, baking soda, and salt. In another bowl, beat the butter and sugar until light and fluffy. Add the egg and vanilla extract and mix until smooth. Gradually add the dry ingredients and mix to form dough.
3. **Cinnamon Swirl:** Roll the dough out on a lightly floured surface into a rectangle about 1/4-inch thick. Sprinkle with cinnamon and brown sugar. Roll the dough tightly, like a cinnamon roll, and cut into 1/2-inch slices.
4. **Bake:** Place the slices on the baking sheet and bake for 8-10 minutes until golden brown. Let cool on a wire rack.

Buttery Vanilla Bean Cookies

Ingredients:

- 2 1/4 cups all-purpose flour
- 1 tsp baking powder
- 1/2 tsp salt
- 1 cup unsalted butter, softened
- 3/4 cup granulated sugar
- 1 large egg
- 1 vanilla bean, scraped (or 1 tsp vanilla extract)
- 1/4 cup powdered sugar (for dusting)

Instructions:

1. **Preheat the Oven:** Preheat your oven to 350°F (175°C). Line a baking sheet with parchment paper.
2. **Make the Dough:** In a bowl, whisk together the flour, baking powder, and salt. In another bowl, beat the butter and sugar until creamy. Add the egg and vanilla bean seeds (or extract) and mix until combined. Gradually add the dry ingredients and mix until a dough forms.
3. **Shape and Bake:** Roll the dough into balls and place them on the baking sheet. Flatten each ball slightly with the bottom of a glass. Bake for 10-12 minutes until golden. Cool slightly, then dust with powdered sugar.

Pumpkin Spice Cookies

Ingredients:

- 2 cups all-purpose flour
- 1/2 tsp baking soda
- 1 tsp ground cinnamon
- 1/2 tsp ground nutmeg
- 1/4 tsp ground ginger
- 1/4 tsp salt
- 1/2 cup unsalted butter, softened
- 1 cup granulated sugar
- 1 large egg
- 1/2 cup pumpkin puree
- 1 tsp vanilla extract
- 1 cup white chocolate chips (optional)

Instructions:

1. **Preheat the Oven:** Preheat your oven to 350°F (175°C). Line a baking sheet with parchment paper.
2. **Make the Dough:** In a bowl, whisk together the flour, baking soda, cinnamon, nutmeg, ginger, and salt. In another bowl, beat the butter and sugar until fluffy. Add the egg, pumpkin puree, and vanilla extract and mix well. Gradually add the dry ingredients and mix until combined. Stir in white chocolate chips if using.
3. **Shape and Bake:** Drop spoonfuls of dough onto the baking sheet. Bake for 10-12 minutes or until golden brown. Let cool on a wire rack.

Chocolate Pudding Cookies

Ingredients:

- 2 1/4 cups all-purpose flour
- 1 tsp baking soda
- 1/2 tsp salt
- 1 package (3.4 oz) instant chocolate pudding mix
- 1 cup unsalted butter, softened
- 3/4 cup granulated sugar
- 3/4 cup packed brown sugar
- 2 large eggs
- 1 tsp vanilla extract
- 2 cups semisweet chocolate chips

Instructions:

1. **Preheat the Oven:** Preheat your oven to 350°F (175°C). Line a baking sheet with parchment paper.
2. **Make the Dough:** In a bowl, whisk together the flour, baking soda, salt, and pudding mix. In another bowl, beat the butter, granulated sugar, and brown sugar until smooth. Add the eggs and vanilla extract, and mix until combined. Gradually add the dry ingredients and mix until fully incorporated. Stir in the chocolate chips.
3. **Shape and Bake:** Drop rounded spoonfuls of dough onto the prepared baking sheet. Bake for 10-12 minutes until the edges are golden. Let cool on a wire rack.

Coconut-Lime Biscuits

Ingredients:

- 2 cups all-purpose flour
- 1/4 cup shredded coconut
- 1/2 tsp baking powder
- 1/4 tsp salt
- 1/4 cup unsalted butter, chilled and cubed
- 1/4 cup granulated sugar
- 1/2 cup buttermilk
- Zest of 1 lime
- 1 tbsp fresh lime juice

Instructions:

1. **Preheat the Oven:** Preheat your oven to 400°F (200°C). Line a baking sheet with parchment paper.
2. **Make the Dough:** In a bowl, whisk together the flour, coconut, baking powder, and salt. Cut in the chilled butter using a pastry cutter or your fingers until the mixture resembles coarse crumbs. Stir in the sugar, lime zest, and lime juice. Gradually add the buttermilk, stirring until a dough forms.
3. **Shape and Bake:** Turn the dough out onto a floured surface and gently knead it. Pat the dough into a 1-inch thick rectangle and cut it into squares or circles. Place the biscuits on the baking sheet and bake for 12-15 minutes, until golden brown. Serve warm.

Pistachio-Rose Water Cookies

Ingredients:

- 1 1/2 cups all-purpose flour
- 1/2 tsp baking powder
- 1/4 tsp salt
- 1/2 cup unsalted butter, softened
- 1/2 cup powdered sugar
- 1 tbsp rose water
- 1/2 tsp vanilla extract
- 1/2 cup shelled pistachios, chopped
- 1 tbsp finely chopped dried rose petals (optional)

Instructions:

1. **Preheat the Oven:** Preheat your oven to 350°F (175°C). Line a baking sheet with parchment paper.
2. **Make the Dough:** In a bowl, whisk together the flour, baking powder, and salt. In another bowl, beat the butter and powdered sugar until smooth. Add the rose water and vanilla extract, and mix well. Gradually add the dry ingredients and mix until a dough forms. Stir in the chopped pistachios and dried rose petals, if using.
3. **Shape and Bake:** Roll the dough into small balls and place them on the baking sheet. Flatten each ball slightly with the back of a spoon. Bake for 10-12 minutes, or until the edges are lightly golden. Cool on a wire rack.

Apple Cinnamon Cookies

Ingredients:

- 2 cups all-purpose flour
- 1 tsp baking soda
- 1/2 tsp ground cinnamon
- 1/4 tsp salt
- 1/2 cup unsalted butter, softened
- 3/4 cup granulated sugar
- 1 large egg
- 1 tsp vanilla extract
- 1/2 cup finely chopped apple (peeled and cored)
- 1/4 cup rolled oats
- 1/2 cup raisins (optional)

Instructions:

1. **Preheat the Oven:** Preheat your oven to 350°F (175°C). Line a baking sheet with parchment paper.
2. **Make the Dough:** In a bowl, whisk together the flour, baking soda, cinnamon, and salt. In another bowl, beat the butter and sugar until smooth. Add the egg and vanilla extract, and mix well. Gradually add the dry ingredients, then stir in the apple, oats, and raisins (if using).
3. **Shape and Bake:** Drop spoonfuls of dough onto the baking sheet. Bake for 10-12 minutes, or until the cookies are golden brown. Let cool on a wire rack.

Salted Caramel Cookies

Ingredients:

- 2 cups all-purpose flour
- 1/2 tsp baking soda
- 1/4 tsp salt
- 1/2 cup unsalted butter, softened
- 1 cup brown sugar, packed
- 1 large egg
- 1 tsp vanilla extract
- 1/2 cup caramel bits or chopped caramel candies
- Sea salt, for sprinkling

Instructions:

1. **Preheat the Oven:** Preheat your oven to 350°F (175°C). Line a baking sheet with parchment paper.
2. **Make the Dough:** In a bowl, whisk together the flour, baking soda, and salt. In another bowl, beat the butter and brown sugar until light and fluffy. Add the egg and vanilla extract, and mix until smooth. Gradually add the dry ingredients, then stir in the caramel bits.
3. **Shape and Bake:** Drop rounded spoonfuls of dough onto the baking sheet. Sprinkle lightly with sea salt. Bake for 10-12 minutes, or until golden brown. Let cool on a wire rack.

Chocolate Toffee Cookies

Ingredients:

- 2 cups all-purpose flour
- 1/2 tsp baking soda
- 1/4 tsp salt
- 1/2 cup unsalted butter, softened
- 3/4 cup brown sugar, packed
- 1/4 cup granulated sugar
- 1 large egg
- 1 tsp vanilla extract
- 1 cup chocolate chips
- 1/2 cup toffee bits

Instructions:

1. **Preheat the Oven:** Preheat your oven to 350°F (175°C). Line a baking sheet with parchment paper.
2. **Make the Dough:** In a bowl, whisk together the flour, baking soda, and salt. In another bowl, beat the butter, brown sugar, and granulated sugar until smooth. Add the egg and vanilla extract, and mix until combined. Gradually add the dry ingredients, then stir in the chocolate chips and toffee bits.
3. **Shape and Bake:** Drop rounded spoonfuls of dough onto the baking sheet. Bake for 10-12 minutes, or until golden brown. Let cool on a wire rack.